VINCENT VAN GOGH

VINCENT VAN GOGH

ODYSSEYS

VALERIE BODDEN

CREATIVE EDUCATION · CREATIVE PAPERBACKS

Published by Creative Education and Creative Paperbacks
P.O. Box 227, Mankato, Minnesota 56002
Creative Education and Creative Paperbacks are imprints of
The Creative Company
www.thecreativecompany.us

Book design by Blue Design (www.bluedes.com)
Art direction by Rita Marshall
Printed in China

Photographs by Alamy (AA World Travel Library, Peter Horree, The Print
Collector, Visual Arts Library-London); The Bridgeman Art Library (Vincent van
Gogh); Corbis (Archivo Iconografico S.A., Christie's Images, Japack Company,
Francis G. Mayer); Getty Images (Allan Tannenbaum/Time Life Pictures,
Imagno/Austrian Archives, Jean-Francois Millet, Vincent van Gogh); The
Granger Collection, New York

Library of Congress Cataloging-in-Publication Data
Bodden, Valerie.
Vincent van Gogh / Valerie Bodden.
p. cm. — (Odysseys in artistry)
Includes bibliographical references and index.
Summary: A biography of Dutch artist Vincent van Gogh, examining his
contributions to the Post-Impressionist style and his early death, as well as
many of his greatest paintings.

ISBN 978-1-60818-721-8 (hardcover)
ISBN 978-1-62832-317-7 (pbk)
ISBN 978-1-56660-756-8 (eBook)
1. Gogh, Vincent van, 1853–1890—Juvenile literature. 2. Painters—Netherlands—
Biography—Juvenile literature.

ND653.G7 B63 2016
759.9492—dc23   2015048531

CCSS: RI.8.1, 2, 3, 4; RI.9-10.1, 2, 3, 4; RI.11-12.1, 2, 3, 4; RH.6-8.1, 4, 5, 7;
RH.9-10.1, 3, 4

First Edition HC 9 8 7 6 5 4 3 2 1
First Edition PBK 9 8 7 6 5 4 3 2 1

CONTENTS

Entering the Art World

Despite the fact that he had never sold a painting, in 1885, Vincent van Gogh confidently told a friend that he needn't sign his artwork, boasting, "[People] will surely recognize my work later on and write about me when I am dead and gone." Although he would go on to sell only one painting in his lifetime, Vincent was right. After his death at the age of 37, his

OPPOSITE: Even though van Gogh somewhat disliked its finished form, *The Starry Night* (1889) has since become his most recognizable work of art.

works—and the story of his tormented life—captured the attention of people around the world, who began to offer extraordinary prices for his paintings. Today, van Gogh's works—some signed with the simple name "Vincent," others left unsigned—are among the most recognizable and valuable pieces of art in the world, drawing crowds of admirers wherever they are exhibited.

Vincent Willem van Gogh was born on March 30, 1853, in the small village of Groot-Zundert, Holland (the Netherlands), the second child of that name to be born to Theodorus and Anna Carbentus van Gogh. Exactly a year before, Anna had delivered a stillborn son, also christened Vincent, now buried in the cemetery of the church where Theodorus served as pastor.

Theodorus hailed from a long line of pastors, but as a minister of the Protestant Dutch Reformed Church serving on the border of Flanders, a primarily Catholic region in northern Belgium, he was never a terribly successful preacher. Nevertheless, from him, Vincent learned to regard his fellow human beings with respect. From his mother, an amateur artist who often drew plants and flowers, Vincent inherited a love of nature and of art.

s a boy, Vincent enjoyed making up games for his two younger brothers and three younger sisters, but he also spent much time alone, rambling through the fields of his native land, gathering beetles

and birds' nests. The scenery of the southern Nether-lands—with its flat horizons, soft gray tones, brown earth, and hardworking peasants—made a lasting impression on Vincent, and he often drew the landscapes, houses, and plants he came across. His family was impressed by his skill. Too impressed, Vincent thought. Once, when he thought his parents had given too much praise to a clay elephant he had molded, he smashed it to pieces; another time, he ripped up an over-admired drawing of a cat. This obstinacy would continue to manifest itself throughout Vincent's life.

Drawing was not Vincent's only interest. He loved to read and thought a love for literature was "sacred." As a result, he spent time memorizing long excerpts from his favorite works by Harriet Beecher Stowe and Charles Dickens. This love of reading also translated into a love of writing—in his lifetime, Vincent would write more than 800 letters, mostly to his brother Theo, revealing the intimate details of his life and work.

incent spent the first years of his education at the village school, but his parents soon feared that he would become coarse from spending so much time with the village's peasant children. As a result, they hired a governess to teach Vincent and his siblings at home. Then, when Vincent was 11, his parents sent him away to a boarding school in the nearby village of Zevenbergen,

where he worked hard but was an average student. Two years later, Vincent was moved to a new school in nearby Tilburg, where he studied a wide range of subjects, including Dutch, German, French, English, arithmetic, history, geography, geometry, botany, zoology, gymnastics, and drawing. The shy and homesick adolescent, whom his sister Elizabeth described as having reddish hair, eyes that "were sometimes blue, sometimes green," and a forehead that "was already slightly wrinkled, his eyebrows drawn together in deep thought," was quiet and unsociable at school.

In 1868, at the age of 15, Vincent left school and spent a year at home with his family. In July of the next year, he left home once again, not to continue his schooling but to begin earning a living. This time, his destination was The Hague, the elegant city that served

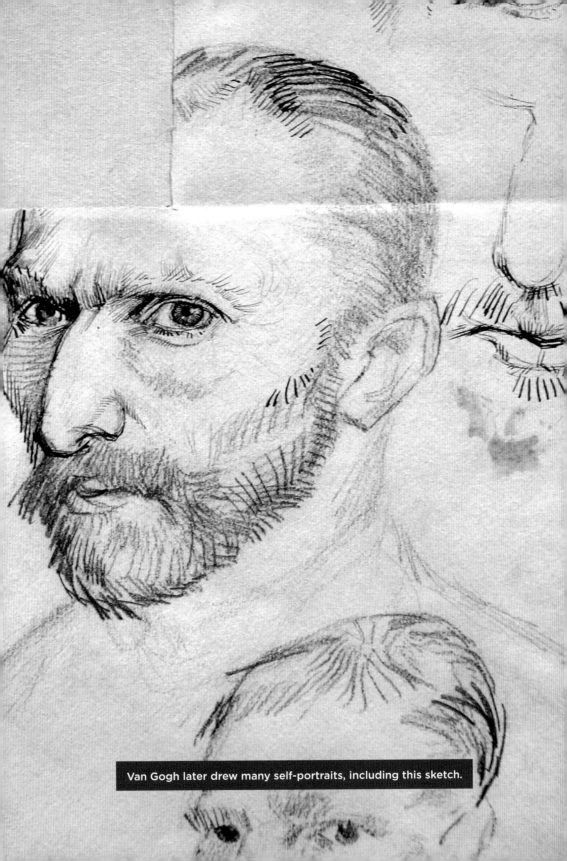

Van Gogh later drew many self-portraits, including this sketch.

"In spite of the sometimes baffling strangeness of his work, it is difficult, for anyone who wants to be objective and who knows how to see, to deny or dispute the simple truth of his art, the ingeniousness of his vision."

— Albert Aurier, French art critic, in the first published article on van Gogh's work as the governmental seat of the Netherlands. There, his uncle Vincent, one of several art dealers in the family, secured him a position as an apprentice at The Hague branch of Goupil, an international art firm that specialized in selling not only original paintings but also **etchings**, **lithographs**, and **prints**. These new innovations made art affordable for the middle class for the first time.

Vincent quickly adapted to his new position, spending most of his free time looking at a broad range of art rather than socializing. At work, both customers and painters said they enjoyed working with Vincent, and his eagerness to succeed in the art trade soon paid off, earning him an outstanding report. In January 1873, he was transferred to the Brussels branch of Goupil, and in June, he was promoted to the company's London branch, beginning a long series of moves across Europe.

Finding His Calling

After arriving in London in June 1873, Vincent immediately purchased a new top hat and a pair of gloves, items that, he wrote his parents, were necessary in England. In his spare time, the 20-year-old explored the city, perusing London's museums, acquainting himself with British art, and sketching the people he encountered.

During his stay in London, Vincent fell in love with Eugenie Loyer, his landlady's daughter, and was deeply

OPPOSITE: A number of van Gogh's defining works, such as *Wheatfield with Cypresses* (1889), feature swirling paint strokes in earthy colors.

hurt when he learned that his love was not reciprocated. As a result of this disappointment, Vincent became moody and irritable, and he refused to go out. Soon, people began to call him eccentric, a label that would be applied to him more and more as time went on.

In October 1874, Vincent was transferred once again, this time to Goupil's headquarters in Paris. There, he spent time in the city's many museums and galleries and also began to attend church services on a regular basis. Although he grew even more interested in art during his time in Paris, Vincent also became disillusioned with the art trade, and it showed in his work. He started to criticize his customers, questioning their taste in art. After a brief return to the London office, he was sent back to Paris, but, with no improvement in his attitude, he was fired in April 1876. Before leaving the city, he went to an exhibition of works by French painter **Jean-François Millet**. He was astounded by what he saw: "When I entered the hall of the Hôtel Drouot, where they were exhibited, I felt like saying, 'Take off your shoes, for the place where you are standing is holy ground.'"

fter his failure in the art business, Vincent moved back to England, where he took up a teaching position at a boarding school on the southeastern coast before moving to a school near London. After less than a year in England, Vincent returned to the Neth-

erlands, where he worked in a bookshop in the town of Dordrecht, spending his spare moments sketching and translating the Bible into French, German, and English as he tried to decide what to do next with his life.

Soon, possibly in an effort to escape loneliness and depression, Vincent decided to become a minister, and in May 1877, at the age of 24, he enrolled in a theology course at the University of Amsterdam. By July 1878, however, Vincent had given up his studies, tired of trying to learn Greek and Latin and eager to begin offering "peace to poor creatures." In August, he left Amsterdam for Laeken, a town near Brussels, Belgium, to enroll in a new training school for lay preachers. After three months, he was allowed to serve on a trial basis as an evangelist in Belgium's coal-mining district known as the Borinage.

n the Borinage, Vincent settled in the mining town of Wasmes. Living among the impoverished miners, the respect for humanity that Vincent had learned from his father filled him with a desire to share in their suffering. He soon left his comfortable quarters at the baker's house and moved into a hut, where he made his bed on a straw mattress. He gave the people of the town all of his possessions, including his own clothes, and stopped washing the coal dust off his face so that he wouldn't stand out from the miners. Although these actions were Vincent's way of trying to act with humility and fit in with the townspeople, he was sometimes regarded with suspicion for his extreme behavior, and many villagers considered him abnormal or a holy fool. Others thought he was mad. In July 1879, he was dismissed from his position.

Vincent then moved to another village, where he again served as a lay preacher, but at the same time, he began to find himself pulled by a renewed interest in drawing. He wrote to his first boss at Goupil and asked him to send some watercolors, a sketchbook, and two instructional books on drawing. Then he set about practicing, working and reworking the lessons in the books and sketching the regions' miners and peasants. Although his progress was slow, sometimes leaving him depressed, he never stopped drawing. He was convinced now that he could serve humanity through art.

The Struggling Artist

Once Vincent decided that he wanted to be an artist, he devoted himself to learning everything he could about drawing and painting. In October 1880, he moved to Brussels, where he applied at the School of Fine Arts but was not accepted. Undeterred, Vincent remained in Brussels, hoping to learn from the artists living there. Because he had no job to support his art interest, Vincent's younger

OPPOSITE: Van Gogh liked to capture, on canvas, the energy of his subjects at work, as illustrated in the 1888 oil painting *Wheatfield with Sheaves*.

brother Theo, who had followed in his footsteps as an art dealer, began to send him a small monthly allowance, which he would continue to provide until the end of Vincent's life.

espite his brother's support, Vincent soon ran out of money, so in April 1881, the 28-year-old returned to his parents' home, now in Etten, the Netherlands. While there, he continued to pursue his art, often working through the night. During this time, Vincent departed from the ways of his contemporaries,

who often pictured peasants at prayer, and decided to show his compassion for the hardworking country people by drawing them as they went about their labor.

During the summer of 1881, Vincent's widowed cousin Kee Vos-Stricker stayed with the family, and Vincent found himself falling in love with her. When he confessed his feelings, however, he again found his love unreturned. Despite this, Vincent continued to pursue Kee, causing tensions in the family, and by the end of the year, he left his parents' house for The Hague.

When he arrived there, Vincent sought art instruction from **Anton Mauve**, a cousin by marriage and one of the foremost members of **The Hague School**, a group of artists who worked toward making painting more modern. Although Vincent was influenced by Mauve's paintings of rural life, his own work from this time featured both rural and urban subjects. For the first time, Vincent attempted to render his subjects in paint; before this, he had concentrated solely on drawing. His first paintings—*Still Life with Cabbage and Clogs* (1881) and *Still Life with Beer Mug and Fruit* (1881)—were rough and not particularly exciting, but they were a starting point.

While living in The Hague, Vincent also pursued romance once again. In March 1882, a pregnant prostitute named Clasina Hoornik (also known as Sien) moved in with him. Sien was a willing subject for Vincent's artwork, posing for around 60 drawings and watercolors. Although Vincent thought about marrying Sien, in September 1883, he left her—and The Hague—for Drenthe, a poor region in the northern Netherlands, looking for an opportunity to be alone with nature and his work. After only a couple of months in this isolated region, Vincent was overcome by loneliness and again packed his bags and headed home to see his parents, who had moved to the town of Nuenen.

s he had done everywhere he had settled since deciding to become an artist, Vincent focused his efforts in Nuenen on his work. His primary subjects became the town's farmers and weavers, as well as dark landscapes featured in such works as *The Vicarage Garden at Nuenen, under Snow* (1885) and *Cottage at Nightfall* (1885). In addition to concentrating on his own

works, Vincent took on three students, accepting tubes of paint as payment. When his students remarked that his painting method—which involved painting quickly, using a large brush and even his fingernails to get the right look—was not in line with academic teachings, he replied, "I scoff at your technique!"

In Nuenen, Vincent again fell in love. This time, he and the woman, Margot Begemann, decided to marry, but when her family objected, she attempted to commit suicide. Less than a year later, in March 1885, Vincent's father died suddenly. Afterward, Vincent set out to paint the cemetery where his father was buried, trying to convey the idea that death and burial were as simple as "the falling of an autumn leaf."

Soon after his father's death, Vincent moved out of his mother's house. He wrote to his brother Theo, "Mother is unable to grasp the idea that painting is a *faith*, and that it imposes the duty to disregard public opinion." Within the next two months, Vincent's faith in his own merits as a painter would finally pay off, as he produced his first work worthy of being called a masterpiece.

The Potato Eaters

Although Vincent was known for working quickly, at times finishing a painting in just a day, he spent more than a month on his first masterpiece, longer than he ever again spent on another picture. He intended, though, for this to be his first important piece and wanted to get it just right. The idea for his first large canvas (measuring 28.5 by 37 inches, or 72.4 by 94 cm) actually came to him in the winter of 1884, although he didn't

OPPOSITE: Van Gogh sometimes included detailed ink sketches, such as this early drawing of *The Potato Eaters*, in the middle of his letters to family members.

begin painting it until April 1885. In the meantime, Vincent spent his days preparing for his ambitious endeavor by drawing and painting studies, or practice pieces.

or his masterpiece, Vincent envisioned a family of peasants sitting around a table, eating potatoes. As he wrote to his brother Theo, "By witnessing peasant life continually, at all hours of the day, I have become so absorbed in it that I hardly ever think of anything else." In order to figure out how to portray the peasants in his painting, Vincent spent many hours in the cottage of one peasant

family in particular, the De Groots. The De Groots amiably accepted their painter friend and allowed him to paint or draw them whenever they weren't working. Often, Vincent focused on drawing their hands and faces, concentrating on every detail. Finally, after spending the whole winter on these studies, he felt as if he could recreate the peasants on the canvas from memory: "I have such a feel of the thing that I can literally dream it."

In early April 1885, Vincent set his brush to the canvas and painted the first strokes of what would come to be known as *The Potato Eaters*. He worked in a small, dark room that he rented from the caretaker of Nuenen's Catholic church. Although he had studied the De Groots in detail before beginning his painting, if he came to a feature he was uncertain of, he grabbed his canvas and rushed to their home, determined to get everything right.

As he worked, Vincent filled his **palette** with the dark colors typical of the 17th-century Dutch paintings he had studied and admired. By painting a single oil lamp above the family's table, he was able to illuminate each of the family members' faces while casting the background details in shadow, highlighting his respect for this hardworking group. Vincent carefully exaggerated the peasants' facial features, calling attention to their strength and the love they expressed for one another over this simple meal of potatoes and coffee. He also made their limbs longer than they would be in real life as a way of bestowing greater importance on his humble subjects, while at the same time trying "to make it clear how those people, eating their potatoes under the lamplight, have dug the earth with those very hands they put into the dish." In painting all of these details, Vincent intentionally left his brushwork rough, explaining, "It would be wrong to give a peasant picture a certain conventional smoothness. If a peasant picture smells of bacon, smoke, potato steam—that's not unhealthy ... to be perfumed is not what a peasant picture needs.... We must continue to give something real and honest."

ven before he had finished *The Potato Eaters*, Vincent knew he had a great work of art on his hands, and he sent his brother Theo many of his early studies, as well as a preliminary print of the work, telling him to keep every-

thing so they wouldn't have to worry about tracking it down and buying it back when he became famous. Theo wasn't quite so confident that the painting would bring Vincent fame, though. He wrote back to Vincent saying that the Impressionists in Paris were using much lighter colors than Vincent had used and that he was going to have to make use of a lighter palette to make it in Paris. Others who saw the painting criticized it as "clumsy." Despite such comments, Vincent was confident that, at the age of 32, he had finally created a masterpiece. Time would prove him right: after his death, *The Potato Eaters* would be considered among the great paintings of the 19th century.

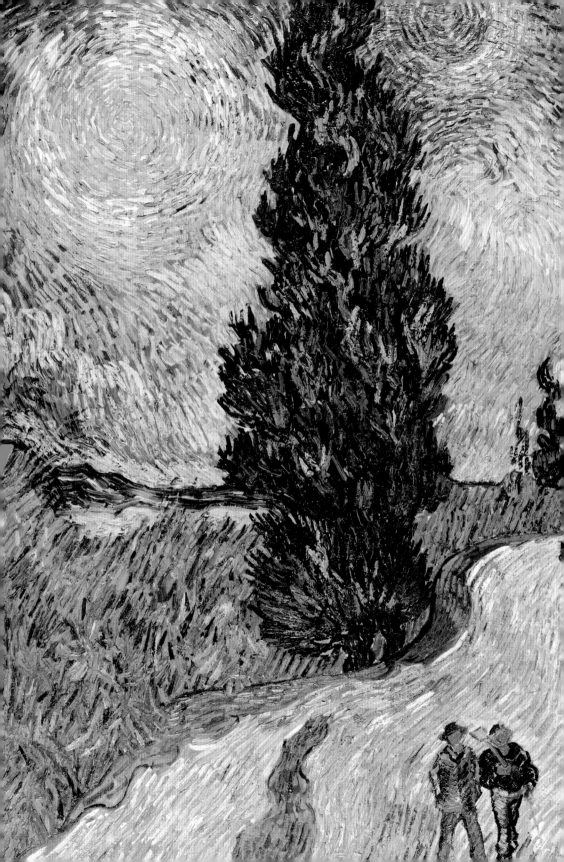

An Early End

After completing *The Potato Eaters*, Vincent felt more confident in his artistic abilities, and in November 1885, he moved to Antwerp, Belgium, and enrolled in the Academy of Fine Arts. Although his fellow students laughed at his unconventional style of quickly slathering on heavy layers of paint, Vincent ignored them. He called their portraits, in which they tried to neatly match the colors and textures of real life, "painfully flat."

OPPOSITE: Van Gogh was fascinated by the forms of cypress trees, and he featured them in many of his works, including *Road with Cypresses* (1890).

In March 1886, Vincent decided to move in with his brother Theo in Paris. Suddenly, he was at the center of the art world, and he soon met some of the great artists of the day, including Camille Pissarro, Paul Signac, and Paul Gauguin. Although the Impressionist movement was declining as Vincent arrived in Paris, Impressionist works, with their light colors and broken brushstrokes, had a strong influence on him, and he began experimenting with a lighter palette in paintings such as *The Gardens of Montmartre* (1887).

Although he enjoyed the atmosphere of Paris, two years of hard living there—drinking and carousing all night—took their toll on Vincent, and by 1888, he was ready for a quieter locale. He chose the town of Arles in southern France. The next 15 months, from February 1888 to May 1889, were the most prolific of Vincent's life, as he produced nearly 200 paintings and more than 100 drawings and watercolors.

uring his time in Arles, Vincent focused on color, believing that "color expresses something in itself." Throughout the spring, he painted bright orchards and flowers. At harvest time, he concentrated on ripe wheat fields, using intense colors and trying to reach what he called the "high yellow note"—the blending of color and emotion to touch his viewers with a sense of life and energy. He finally felt that he achieved this

with *Harvest at La Crau* (1888), a vivid painting of the fields surrounding Arles. In the winter, Vincent turned to painting portraits of his neighbors. Even in these pictures, he placed an emphasis on color, seeking to portray not reality, but feeling—love for a friend or respect for a peasant. With his attempts to create emotion on the canvas, Vincent became one of the forerunners of **Expressionism**.

In October 1888, Vincent was joined by fellow artist Paul Gauguin. The two soon began to fight about their differing views of art, however, and Vincent started to act oddly, becoming rough and loud and then lapsing into silence. On December 23, Vincent allegedly threatened Gauguin with a razor, and Gauguin fled. Afterward—in a fit of madness or drunkenness—Vincent used the razor to cut off part of his own left ear. The next day, he was taken to the hospital, where he remained on and off over the next few months, suffering from delusions and depression.

In May 1889, Vincent left Arles for the asylum of Saint-Rémy, about 20 miles (32.2 km) away. Although occasional psychological attacks—possibly caused by an unusual form of epilepsy—rendered him unable to work, in between these fits, Vincent created more than 100 canvases and as many drawings. Among these was what is today one of his most famous paintings, *The Starry Night* (1889), with its swirling sky, mysterious stars, and flamelike cypress trees. While he was at Saint-Rémy, Vincent also sold his first painting—the only one he sold during his lifetime. In February 1890, *The Red Vineyard* (1888) brought him about $80 (the equivalent of approximately $1,000 today).

n May, Vincent left Saint-Rémy for the city of Auvers-sur-Oise, near Paris, where he again worked feverishly. Although he felt that the countryside held "restorative forces," Vincent also suffered periods of great loneliness there. On July 23, 1890, he wrote, "This misery will never end." Four days later, on July 27, he walked into a field with a revolver and shot himself. He died two days later, at the age of 37. After a funeral attended by friends, family, and fellow artists, Vincent was buried in Auvers. He had come to art late and left it early, but after his death, his works lived on, becoming some of the most famous in the world and causing millions of viewers to catch their breath in awe. And in the end, that's what Vincent wanted: to touch people through his art.

VINCENT VAN GOGH

In His Words

Vincent van Gogh was a prolific and gifted writer who, throughout his life, sent hundreds of letters to his brother Theo, as well as to other family members and friends. More than 800 of these letters survive, and they give us insight into the writer's personal and professional life. In the excerpts that follow, all taken from letters written by Vincent to Theo, he reveals his thoughts about art as well as about himself and his relation to the world around him.

OPPOSITE: Van Gogh was one of his own best subjects; he produced many self-portraits, including *Self-Portrait with Grey Felt Hat* (1887–88).

55

The following excerpt from a letter written in The Hague in July 1882 explains what van Gogh saw as his purpose in art, as well as his perception of how the world viewed him.

I want to make drawings that touch people. "Sorrow" is a modest beginning; perhaps such little landscapes as the "Meerdervoort Avenue," the "Ryswyk Meadows," and "Fish-Drying Barn" are also a slight beginning. But in these there is at least something that has come directly from my own heart.

Either through figures or through landscapes I wish to express, not sentimental melancholy, but serious sorrow. In short, I want to reach so far that people will say of my work: He feels deeply, he feels tenderly—notwithstanding my so-called roughness, perhaps even because of it.

"I am convinced that if he has a few more years he will make a name for himself.... He is one of the pioneers of the new ideas, or rather he is trying to revive ideas that have been falsified in routine everyday life and have lost their luster."

— Theo van Gogh, Vincent's brother

It seems pretentious now to speak so, but that is the reason that I want to push on with full strength. What am I in the eyes of most people? A good-for-nothing, an eccentric and disagreeable man, somebody who has no position in society and never will have. Very well, even if that were true, I should want to show by my work what there is in the heart of such an eccentric man, of such a nobody.

This is my ambition, which is founded less on anger than on love, founded more on serenity than on passion. It is true that I am often in the greatest misery, but still there is within me a calm, pure harmony and music. In the poorest huts, in the dirtiest corner, I see drawings and pictures. And with irresistible force my mind is drawn towards these things. Believe me that sometimes I laugh heartily because people suspect me of all kinds of malignity and absurdity, of which not a hair of my head is guilty—I,

VINCENT VAN GOGH

who am really no one but a friend of nature, of study, of work, and especially of people.

In this excerpt from a letter written in Nuenen in July 1885, van Gogh talks about his distaste for artistic "technique" and discusses what he thinks art should be.

I have here before me some figures; a woman with a spade seen from behind; another bending to glean the corn ears; another seen from the front, her head almost on the ground, digging carrots; a woman winding sheaves. I have been watching these peasant figures here for more than a year and a half, especially their action, just to catch their character.

The time is gone when it was sufficient for a figure to be academically, conventionally correct; or rather, though many still ask for this, a reaction is coming. The artists are

"He never seems to be learning from his art. From the very first his conviction in what he has to say is intense enough to carry him through all the difficulties, hesitations, and doubts which beset the learner. He works ... with a feverish haste to get the image which obsesses him externalized in paint."

— Roger Fry, English art critic, in an article from 1923

calling for character; well—the public will do the same.

These Moorish, Spanish things, cardinals, all these historical paintings which they keep on painting and painting, yards upon yards, what is the use of it, and why do they do it? After a few years it gets musty and dull, and more and more uninteresting. Well! Perhaps they are well painted; they may be. But nowadays when critics stand before a picture such as one of [French painter] Benjamin Constant's or a reception at the cardinal's by I don't know what Spaniard, it is the custom to speak with a philosophical air about "clever technique."

I care less and less for that so highly praised but so inexpressibly dreadfully dry technique of the Italians and Spaniards. Now, I ask you: What kind of man, what kind of prophet, or philosopher, or observer, what kind of human character is there behind certain paintings the technique of which is praised? In fact, often nothing. But standing before many pictures of almost unknown artists one feels they are made with a will, a feeling, a passion, and love. And if one considers these things, am I then so far wrong when I criticize the criticism of those critics who in these days talk humbug about this so often misused word, "technique"? With the selfsame air these very critics would come before a picture of rural life and would criticize the "technique."

The technique of a painting from rural life, or of one, such as [French painter Jean-François] Raffaëlli's, from the heart of the city workmen, presents quite other difficulties than those of the smooth painting and pose of a [Gustave Jean] Jacquet or a Benjamin Constant. In Paris all kinds of Arabic and Spanish and Moorish models are to be had if one only pays for them, but he who paints the

rag-pickers of Paris, in their own quarter, has far more difficulties and his work is more serious.

You think perhaps I am wrong to criticize this, but it strikes me that all those foreign pictures are painted in the studio.

But go and paint out-of-doors on the spot itself! Then all kinds of things happen. From the four paintings which you will receive, I had to wipe off at least a hundred and more flies; not counting the dust and sand; not counting that when one carries them for some hours across the heath and through the hedges, some thorns will scratch them; not counting that when one arrives on the heath after some hours' walk in the weather, one is tired and exhausted from the heat; not counting that the figures do not stand still like professional models, and the effects one wants to catch change with the passing day.

To paint direct from life means to live in those cottages day by day, to be in the fields as are the peasants; in summer to stand the heat of the sun, in winter to suffer from snow and frost, not indoors but outside, and not just during a walk, but day after day like the peasants themselves.

Apparently nothing is simpler than to paint peasants, rag-pickers, and labourers of all kinds, but—no subjects in painting are so difficult as these everyday figures.

So far as I know there is not a single academy where one can learn to draw and paint a digger, a sower, a woman who puts the kettle over the fire, or a seamstress. But in every city there is an academy with a choice of models for historical, Arabic, Louis XV figures—none of them with any real existence.

When I send to you and [French painter Charles] Serret some studies of diggers or peasant women who weed or

glean, it may be that either you or he will discover faults in them, of which it will be useful for me to know. But I want to point out something which is worthwhile. All academical figures are constructed in the same way—irreproachably faultless. They do not reveal to us anything new.

A drawing of a peasant woman by a Parisian who has learned drawing at the Academy will always indicate the limbs and the structure of the body in one selfsame way, sometimes charming—correct in proportion and anatomy. But when [Dutch painter Jozef] Israëls, or [French painter Honoré] Daumier or [French painter Léon-Augustin] Lhermitte, or especially [French painter Eugène] Delacroix, draws a figure, the shape of the figure will be felt much more, yet the proportions will sometimes be almost arbitrary, the anatomy and structure often quite wrong "in the eyes of the academician." But the figure will live.

Rather than to say there must be character in a digger, I circumscribe this by saying that the peasant must be a peasant, that the digger must dig, and then there will be something essentially modern in them—then a figure will not be superfluous. To draw a figure in action, that implies an essentially modern figure, the very heart of modern art, which neither the Greeks nor the Renaissance nor the old Dutch school have done.

In August 1888, Vincent wrote the following from Arles about the use of color to portray feelings and ideas in portraits.

What a mistake Parisians make in not having a palate for crude things! But there, what I learnt in Paris is leaving me, and I am returning to the ideas I had in the

"Vincent and I rarely agree on much, least of all where painting is concerned.... He likes my paintings very much, but when I am at work on them he is forever saying that I am doing things wrong somewhere or other."

— French artist Paul Gauguin

country before I knew the impressionists. And I should not be surprised if the impressionists find fault with my way of working, for it has been fertilized by the ideas of Delacroix rather than by theirs. I use color more arbitrarily so as to express myself forcibly. Well, let that be as far as theory goes, but I am going to give you an example of what I mean.

I should like to paint the portrait of an artist friend, a man who dreams great dreams, who works as the nightin-gale sings, because it is in his nature. He'll be a fair man. I want to put into my picture my appreciation, the love that I have for him. So I paint him as he is, as faithfully as I can.

But the picture is not finished yet. To finish it I am now going to be the arbitrary colorist. I exaggerate the fairness of the hair; I come even to orange tones, chromes and pale lemon-yellow. Beyond the head, instead of painting the ordinary wall of the mean room, I paint infinity, a plain background of the richest, intensest blue that I can contrive, and by this simple combination of the bright head against the rich blue background I get a mysterious effect, like a star in the depths of an azure sky.

In the portrait of the peasant, again, I worked in this way, but without wishing in this case to produce the mysterious brightness of a pale star in the infinite. Instead, I think of the man I have to paint as terrible in the furnace of the full harvest, the full South; hence the stormy orange shades, vivid as red-hot iron, and hence the luminous tones of old gold in the shadows.

Oh, my dear boy!—and the nice people will only see the exaggeration as caricature. But what has that to do with us?

Timeline

1853 Vincent Willem van Gogh is born in the village of Groot-Zundert, Holland, on March 30.

1864 Van Gogh is sent away to boarding school, first in Zevenbergen, then, two years later, in Tilburg.

1868 Van Gogh leaves school and returns home for a year.

1869 Van Gogh leaves home for The Hague, where he works as an apprentice at the art firm Goupil.

1873 Goupil transfers van Gogh to Brussels, then London; in London, he is rejected romantically by Eugenie Loyer.

1874 Van Gogh is transferred to Goupil's headquarters in Paris.

1876 After being fired from Goupil, van Gogh moves to England to teach.

1877 Van Gogh enrolls in a theology course at the University of Amsterdam but drops out after a year.

1878 Van Gogh moves to the Borinage mining region in Belgium to serve as a lay preacher.

1880 After deciding to become an artist, van Gogh moves to Brussels, Belgium.

1881 Van Gogh joins his parents in Etten, the Netherlands; he later moves to The Hague, living with Clasina Hoornik.

1883 Van Gogh moves in with his parents in Nuenen, the Netherlands.

1884 Margot Begemann, van Gogh's fiancée, attempts suicide because her family opposes the couple's marriage.

1885 Van Gogh's father dies; he paints his first masterpiece, *The Potato Eaters*.

1886 Van Gogh moves to Paris, where he lives with his brother Theo.

1888 Van Gogh moves to Arles, France; in December, he cuts off part of his left ear.

1889 Van Gogh voluntarily checks into the asylum at Saint-Rémy, France.

1890 Van Gogh sells his first painting; he moves to Auvers-sur-Oise, where he shoots himself on July 27, dying two days later.

Selected Bibliography

Greenberg, Jan, and Sandra Jordan. *Vincent van Gogh: Portrait of an Artist*. New York: Delacorte Press, 2001.

Hammacher, A. M. *Van Gogh*. London: Paul Hamlyn, 1967.

Mühlberger, Richard. *What Makes a van Gogh a van Gogh?* New York: The Metropolitan Museum of Art, 1993.

Petrie, Brian. *Van Gogh: Paintings, Drawings, and Prints*. London: Phaidon Press, 1974.

Stone, Irving, ed. *Dear Theo: The Autobiography of Vincent van Gogh*. Garden City, N.Y.: Doubleday, 1946.

Torterolo, Anna. *Van Gogh*. Translated by Sylvia Tombesi-Walton. New York: DK, 1999.

Wallace, Robert. *The World of van Gogh: 1853–1890*. New York: Time-Life Books, 1969.

Whiteley, Linda. *Van Gogh: Life and Works*. Naperville, Ill.: Sourcebooks, 2000.

Glossary

Anton Mauve a 19th-century Dutch painter belonging to The Hague School; most of his works are realistic portrayals of people—especially peasants—and animals in outdoor scenes

Camille Pissarro a 19th-century French painter who exhibited with Claude Monet and other Impressionists; he painted many French landscapes

etchings prints made by cutting lines into a metal plate with acid; the plate is then covered with ink, and a piece of paper is pressed onto it, picking up the ink from the etched lines

Expressionism an artistic movement of the late 19th and early 20th centuries in which artists tried to portray subjective feelings rather than objective reality; the subjects of Expressionist paintings are often distorted in some way to stress emotion

The Hague School a group of artists who met in The Hague from 1860 to 1890; rather than idealizing their subjects as many of their contemporaries did, these artists sought to portray their subjects realistically

Impressionists followers of an artistic movement of the late 19th century, in which painters tried to capture "an impression of the moment" by using disconnected brushstrokes and bright, unmixed colors

Jean-François Millet a 19th-century French painter known for his works of peasants in the fields

lithographs prints made through the process of lithography, in which an artist makes a drawing on a flat plate, then uses a chemical process to make a number of paper copies from the plate

palette a surface—often made of wood, plastic, or tile—on which an artist mixes his paints; the word can also refer to the general set of colors used by an artist

Paul Gauguin a 19th-century French artist whose works are distinguished by large areas of flat color; he helped move art toward Synthetism and Symbolism, in which artists combined reality with elements from dreams

Paul Signac a French painter of the late 19th and early 20th centuries who helped to develop pointillism, a painting technique in which small dots of pure color are placed next to one another, appearing to blend together when seen from a distance

prints works of art made by a printing process, such as etching or engraving, usually on paper; many prints are copies of famous works of art

Index